The Moon is on the

The Wild & Wacky Poems
of
ANDREW FUSEK PETERS

Illustrated by
DANNY BRADFORD

SHERBOURNE PUBLICATIONS

Dedication

To Polly

Acknowledgements

TELEVISION & RADIO

The Moon Is On The Microphone, Rush Hour Rhythm, Last Night I saw The City Breathing, Watch Out, Watch Out, There's A 'Po-Leaf' Car About & Trees Don't Go To School all appeared on BBC1's *Wham! Bam! Strawberry Jam! 1997*

Trees Don't Go To School appeared on *Blue Peter,* 1992
Hey Diddle Diddle was broadcast on *Poetry Please,* 1995

Poem For The Verbally Confused, The Hills Are Alive With The Sound Of Knitting & Last Night I saw The City Breathing were recorded live at the BBC Poetry Festival For Children and broadcast on a Radio 5 *Talking Poetry* Feature 1993

The Magician, Rhythm Of The Day, A Tidy Poem, Hey Diddle Diddle, Snoring, The River Of Tears, School Rhymes & School Times & Rush Hour Rhythm were all recorded live at the BBC Poetry Festival For Children and broadcast on a Radio 4 *Talking Poetry* Feature 1995

PUBLICATIONS

Poem For The Verbally Confused was published in *Custard Pie* (Macmillan) 1996
This poem was also published with *Hey Diddle Diddle* in the Radio 4/Poetry Society *Young Poetry Pack* – 1995
Snoring & *The River Of Tears* were published in *May The Angels Be With Us* Shropshire County Council Education Services 1994
The Dancing Carrot was published in *Sheep Don't Go To School* (Bloodaxe) 1997

A selection of these poems were published in Andrew's first two collections with Sherbourne – *Word-Whys* & *The Weather's Getting Verse*

Contents

THE MOON IS ON THE MICROPHONE 2
THE DANCING CARROT 3
A RECIPE 4
OUT TO LUNCH 5
ED THE DREAMER 6
THE EGG PICKER-UPPER 7
A SAUCY POEM 9
MY CAT SOOTY 10
SNORING 11
THE RIVER OF TEARS 12
THE LEAF'S LAMENT 13
THE GOLD-LEAF GANGSTER 15
WATCH OUT, WATCH OUT,
THERE'S A 'PO-LEAF' CAR ABOUT! 16
TREES DON'T GO TO SCHOOL 17
A POCKET FULL OF PLAY 19
"SNEEZE ALLEGATIONS" 21
SCHOOL RHYMES AND SCHOOL TIMES 23
RHYTHM OF THE DAY 25
POEM FOR THE VERBALLY CONFUSED 27
THE LETTER 29
THE HILLS ARE ALIVE WITH
THE SOUND OF KNITTING 31
THE MAGICIAN 33
MY DAD SAYS HE'S A LOONY 34
THE SAFEST PLACE IN THE WORLD 35
BOB THE YOB (THE BOY WITH NO BRAIN) 36
AND OUR LAST STORY TONIGHT 37
LAST NIGHT, I SAW THE CITY BREATHING 39
RUSH HOUR RHYTHM 41
BALLAD OF THE TREES 43
THE MILK CUP 44
STREET SIGNS 45
THE MANSION 46
NIGHT 47
DAY 48
THE CAT SAT ON THE MAT 49
THE NOUN WITH NO NAME 50
THE HEADBANGING POEM 51
GORILLA 54
THE RUBBISHMAN 55
HEY DIDDLE DIDDLE 57
A TIDY POEM 58
A FAREWELL ODE 59

The Moon is on the Microphone (a country rap)

Oh the trees are dressing for an all night bop
And the sheep are going bonkers as they do the Heron Hop.
And the little leaf sister
How she boogies with the breeze
As the cows do the rhythm
With the spoons on their knees.
All the birds are singin'
On the Top of the Plops
And the wind he is a drumming
With a bunch of carrot tops.
The sheep are looking chic
In the latest woolly style
As they hop a happy conga
In a crocodile file.
And the stars are driven down
From their mansions in the sky,
The clouds would like a dance
But they dare not even try,
So they cry-baby, hey-baby, grumble and sigh!
And the Moon is on the microphone,
Crooning quite a tune
As every blade of grass
Is falling to a swoon.
Wow!
What a bop
'Til you drop
What a sight,
What a night,
What an animal rite!

The Dancing Carrot

The beetroot was getting married,

The celery squealed with delight,

The carrot stood up to dance a jig

And the horseradish whistled all night!

Traditional Czech

A Recipe

Take a bunch of twinkling stars
And grab them by their shiny toes!
Pull them gently down to Earth,
Then stick them up your nose!

OUCH! and OW! They might shout out,
IT'S DARK IN HERE, IT'S HOT!
Wiggle them round with a pair of spoons,
Cover them well with snot!

Then pull them out with your fingers
Until they turn to chewing gum,
Sprinkle them with ear wax,
And squash them with your thumb!

Roll them flat with a rolling pin,
Then turn the oven on.
Ever so quickly shove them in,
And wait until they're done.

Ketchup, plate, sit and wait,
With soggy chips, what a treat!
They're ready, steady, hungry, go!
Yes! Bogey stars are great to eat!

And you might wonder why they're green,
But I can tell you where they've been!

Out to Lunch

A poem in three movements

1.

I'm starving, I'm dying

I need a chip injection!

I've got sausage fever

And vegetable rejection,

2.

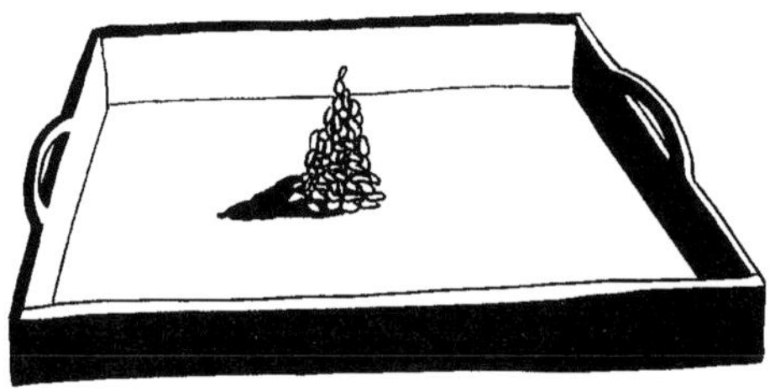

Oh Cauliflowers, boiled for hours

So soft and lumpy grey,

You look just like a bunch of brains

Or snot piled up in a tray!

3.

I'm in love with pudding

And pudding's in love with me,

Give me a smile and a Custard Kiss

And we'll marry at half-past three!

Ed the Dreamer

"If you don't eat your greens right now!" Mum said,

"You'll end up thin as a slice of bread!"

Ed stuffed his face with dreams instead,

Thoughts to crunch and fears that fed

Nightmares into his head,

Got thin as a thread,

Mum cried, and led

Him to bed

Now Ed's

*Dead.........**HUNGRY!***

The Egg Picker-Upper

Which came first,
The egg or the chicken?
Listen to this tale,
And let the plot thicken...

Once on the farm
The chicken scratched,
Found a barn
For eggs to hatch.

Eggs for chicks
And eggs on toast,
Chicken lived well,
A tasty roast.

The farmer smiled,
Though times were hard
As bird ran free
Throughout the yard.

Times changed:

There was a man,
An egg-picker-upper,
He'd never again
Eat eggs for his supper.

Four thousand chickens,
All in one shed,
Some of them squawking,
Some of them dead.

Day was outlawed,
Lightbulb reigned,
Farmer vanished,
Birds well-trained.

Backs scratched raw
Bleeding and sad,
This egg machine
Has gone quite mad.

And when their
Laying days have flown,
A pet food tin
Is their final home.

The chicken, or the egg,
Which came first?
Who really cares,
For the bird that's cursed?

A Saucy Poem

There was a little lamb
With such a golden fleece
"Oops!" Went the butcher
Roast In Peace!

Lamb jumped out of oven
Oh No, he's hopping free!
Hungry butcher bleating,
"It was not *mint* to be!"

My Cat Sooty

When Sooty died,
I felt flat as a football pitch.
Tears kicked out of my eyes,
Dribbled down my face
Into the mouth,
Scoring an own goal.
All play was suspended.

When Sooty died,
My frown
Was turned down
Like a telephone crying
Brrring Brrring Bring me some happiness.
But no-body answered.

When Sooty died,
My heart was sour as old milk.
I was all bottled up inside,
Remembering a pint of purrs,
Creamy whiskers
And Sooty, pouring herself into my lap.
All my days have now gone off.
And there's no silver-top lining in the cloudy sky.

Snoring

My brother's snoring
Makes such a sound!
It shakes the bed
And shivers the ground.
I never get any sleep,
Not even a peep
Because of that creep....

So, I stick my two big toes
Right up his nose!
It's the best way to stop him, I've found!

The River of Tears

Why is there rain, and where does it come from mum?
And how come clouds live up in the sky?
And why did my brother get ill and die?

The rain is a river of tears, my dear,
For every cloud sees how sad we are here.
Yet I don't know why your brother should die.

Why are the leaves so bright and so green mum
And how do they learn to fall off and fly?
And why did my brother get ill and die?

Leaves are alive and filled with breath, my child.
At the end of the year, they have their death.
But I just don't know how my son could die.

And will he ever come back again mum?
And can't we find him if we really try?
And I'm so unhappy mum, why did he die?

He's taken a boat to the river of tears
And we shall not see him for so many years
So hold my hand, little one, and wave him goodbye.
So hold my hand tight, little one, and wave him goodbye.

The Leaf's Lament

Said the leaf to the sky,

I would learn how to fly,

But I'm shaking like a leaf, do I dare?

Said the sky to the leaf,

It's a matter of belief,

Just jump into my blanket of air!

Then the sky sang,

Then the leaf sprang,

And the trees were empty and bare.

The Gold-Leaf Gangster

Autumn:
Summer sighed,
Sat down
And Winter offered her a cup of tea.

Autumn:
Summer's gone,
Took her summer holiday.

Autumn:
Friend of sly Winter,
The Gold-Leaf Gangster.
This man is wanted for tree-stripping
And stealing summer's colour TV.
For the next three months,
It's only black and white.

Autumn:
Summer's so sad
She went for a night out on the town
And afterwards,
Couldn't remember a thing.

Hot and bothered Nature
Bought an air freshener.
But cool Winter got a bit too fresh,
Made his big mistake
When he kissed the sleeping beauty,
Spring!

Watch Out, Watch Out, there's a 'Po-Leaf' Car about!

Leaves are like traffic lights.
On the trunk-road
Of slow-moving seasons,
They go
Green,
Yellow,
Red.
The Summer stops!
The sun is switched off!
The trees become
A multi-coloured traffic jam!

Then,
A crazy wind drives straight through the forest tall,
Makes each and every leaf
To fall and crash
Into the pile-up of Autumn.

And we,
Hoot and holler,
Dive and dash,
Scream and dream
And jump in the mess of shining, twisted leaves.
This happy accident of once a year
Where no-one is hurt, and nobody grieves.

Trees don't go to School

Trees don't go to school,
Won't sit still and shut up
And muck about lots.
Trees are messy, never comb their hair
And once a year
They dare to cover our clean concrete streets
With their dirty brown leaves!
Trees definitely deserve detentions!

Trees keep on growing,
NO matter how much you shout at them
But in the end, just like you
They can be hurt.

"Daydreaming again little Larch?
When the head hears of this
He'll chop you into little bits!
Out with the chainsaw
And little Larchy is no more!
In ten days time you'll be shiny and neat,
Finishing your life as a wooden toilet seat!"

Hang on a second...
Trees have had enough!
We will not be sat on anymore!
TREES ON TRUANT!
We want to wake with the soft dawn,
Let the sun melt us into day,
Hear the birds sing inside us!

TREES ON TRUANT!

If you keep cutting us down,
We'll hold our breath,
Until the world turns blue
And no-one can breathe.

WE INTERRUPT THIS POEM FOR AN EMERGENCY NEWSFLASH!

"Yesterday it was reported that a young beech tree was caught streaking stark naked through the quiet streets of Winter. One blind resident complained, **'Ugh! All those rude branches dancing nude in the wind, with not even a leaf to cover herself! It's disgusting and shouldn't be allowed!'** The government has reacted by issuing a standard set of white cotton underpants to every tree in the country."

A Pocket full of play

Sing a song of schooltime,
A pocket full of play
Four and twenty children
Working through the day.

When the class was over,
The kids began to sing,
Time for fun and a bucket of sun
Until the bell shall ring.

Children in the playground,
Where it's nice and sunny,
Teacher's in the staffroom
Eating bread and honey.
The head is in the office,
Twiddling her toes,
When in came a naughty boy,
Picking at his nose!

"Sneeze allegations!"

TIFF TRINGLE IN SHARP SHOCK!

"Reporter Dan Bogeyman here, nosing about
at Our Lady of the Messy Handbag Infant School.

Disaster struck at eleven-fifteen this morning.

According to eye witness accounts,
pupil Chris Snot-In-Face was seen flicking a pencil sharpener
at naughty boy Japhed-*it-wasn't-me-miss*-Warez.

Chris missed.

The sharpener shot like snot right up Tiffany Tringle's nose.

Screams were heard in Timbuktu!

The Liar-Brigade arrived and Miss Tringle,
aged six-and-three-quarters
underwent an emergency Nostrilectomy,
and is said to be feeling much better.
The sharpener has been charged
with breaking and entering.

This is Dan Bogeyman,
from *The Nose At Ten!*"

DAILY NEWS
4792
75p
HELP
SNEEZE ALLEGATIONS

School Rhymes & School Times

School! Oh! School is a feel-sick-won't-go place,
A stay-at-home-in-case-they-call-me-names-like-*Pasty-Face* place.

School! Oh! School is a can't-cry place,
A don't-show-your-tears-or-they-laugh-in-your-face place.

School! Oh! School is hate-in-wait-outside-the-class place,
A bully-words-of-stick-and-stone-to-break-my-bones place.

School! Oh! School is a teacher-tell-me-off place,
A terrible-case!-Shoes-unlaced!-Hair's-all-over-the-place place.

But,

School! Oh! School is some-days-OK-place,
A best-friend-game-of-hide-and-seek-and-sardines place.

School! Oh! School is a tasty place,
A say-your-grace-yummy-plaice-and-chips-and-peas-please-on-Friday place.

School! Oh! School is an out-of-breath-run-and-play place,
A climb-up-grown-up trees-it's-ace! place

School! Oh! School is an I've-won-first place! place
A best-in-the-race-with-the-fastest-pace-in-the-place place.

Oh! School! Yes! School is a sometimes hot, sometimes cold place,
A-Got-to-go, got-to-grow, get-to-know-it's-not-so-bad-after-all place.

Rhythm of the Day

And the rain and the rain on the window pane,
alarm and awake, and "I'm hungry Mum!"
And the rain and the post and soldiers of toast
with tea.

And me and my brother
and the chatter and the clatter
and the buzz on the bus on the way to school
and smiles and crisps and bags on backs
with books.

And socks in shoes are wet as the sea
and the friends and the class so brightly lit
and we dream and it steams the windows up
and it's safe.

And the rain and the rain and the rain is beating
sleeting, world-defeating.
A cough and a shiver and stamping of feet,
"Oh when will the storm be over?"

And the rain is a pain that has gone away
and the clouds so proud are sulking.
And the day is long and on and on
with sun and fun and hide and seek
'til mum calls out with a cry and a shout.
Oh why do we have to go home?

And we run and pour though lane and door
and the clatter and the chatter of knives and forks
and nice hot food and a big fat tum
and the sun has begun to set.

And a bath and a bath and a simmering bath
poking, joking, everyone's soaking.
A race and a race, first place to bed
and the sky in the night is filled with stars
and the room is full of whispers.
And a sleep and a sleep and it's time to sleep
and a sleep and a sleep and I'm counting sheep
and asleep and asleep and I'm falling deep.

Poem for the Verbally Confused

Got up, Boiled the bed,
Took a train downstairs,
Feeling live-tired and with such a baking head.

Drank not one shredded wheat but three,
Then I Grew myself a nice cup of tea,
Planted some toast, Watered the eggs,
Sat down in a chair and Ate my legs.

Crushed my teeth, Smashed my face,
Poached my hair 'til I Looked dead ace!
Dug my way to school,
And after, Went for a Snog in the local Snogging Pool!

Caught the bus, Put it in my pocket,
My mum Made a fuss and Told me to Return it.
Killed my homework, which Was very satisfying,
Especially when all the answers Were Writhing around and Dying!

In the end, I Pounded into bed,
Cut off my tired and weary head
And Swam down deep into soft and silent sleep...

SNOGGING POOL
THAT
THAN
TO
IS THE
HOMWORK
IT IS
NOT TO BE
ENGLISH WEATHE
TO BE OR

The Letter

Begun with a word
Spun from the heart
To click the pen
And make it start.

Out pours ink
To the alphabet sea,
Whales of words
Racing free.

My words are done
So wrap them tight
In an envelope
Of night.

Stamp a head
Onto its face,
Dressed with address
Slotted in place...

'Til along comes burglar
With sack and key
To steal the words
To you from me.

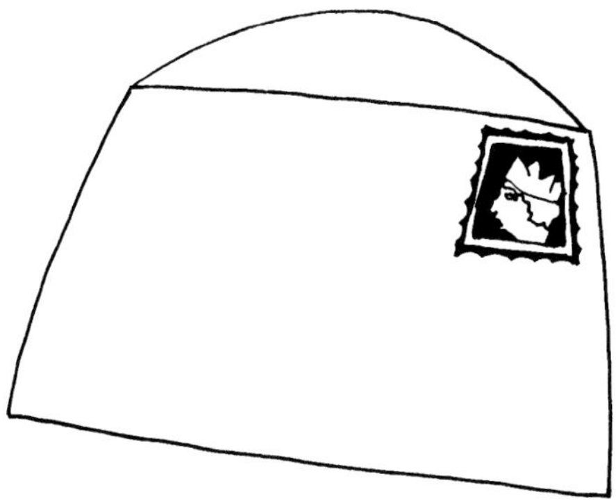

Sack to van
And van to train
Into the night,
Words like rain,

Falling through tunnels
And grumbling towns
Sidings, hiding
Smiles and Frowns.

Slow train, night train
Cradle of words,
Rocking on tracks
Through sleepy suburbs.

Screech to a full stop,
Stationary halted,
Words of the thwarted
Courted, sorted.

Van to Sack
And sack to fist,
Pushed through doors
With a twist of the wrist.

Shepherd Postman,
Delivering herds,
A flock of letters,
Bleating words.

Head feels woolly
At break of day
Here comes the post,
Now what will it say?

Rip the envelope,
Pour out my heart.
Must write back,
But where shall I start?

The Hills are alive with the sound of Knitting

Last night, my Auntie Madge
Knitted a couple of hills.
She got the pattern from a magazine,
KNITTING TODAY!
"For colourful effect, add animals, two or three, say."
So she crocheted a bobble of bleating sheep
And into the hills they creep, they creep.
All night it took my Auntie Madge.

"How about some day"? **She beamed,**
And wove it ray by ray
'Til her fingers were so sore,
But Aunt Madge, she saw
That it was good.

"Next," **said the magazine,** ***"You could try***
A few seam-stitches to cover the sky!"
It seemed she needed her knitting machine,
Took out her Singer, that sang so loud,
Birds awoke, stitch turned to cloud.
Aunt Madge sat back, satisfied,
"I shall call it....Countryside!"

Then along came a man, striding, striding
Wearing a pair of concrete shoes.
"Hear my news!" **he said,**
As he snagged the thread,
And under his tread
Unravelled the land.

The Magician

Blue was the sky, blue as a blade,
Made to cut the clouds from high,
Floating feathers that fell to the sea,
White as a wave with a foaming sigh.

But the sun felt tired, decided to set,
Set down her bed, unfold her quilt
Of strawberry-red. Curled like a flower
She fell into dream and day began to wilt.

Night strolled by, dressed in dark,
With a blanket of black, he blinded the sky,
Clicked his fingers, struck a spark,
And the sky was a pirate with one silver eye.

He took off his hat of infinite deep,
Stars like rabbits shot from their sleep.
From his sleeves came a handkerchief, soft and grey,
With a flourish it shimmered as the Milky Way.

How the trees clapped for Magician Night!
How the sea cried one foaming tear!
Now the hills sing in his shadowy light,
Now the land waits for day to draw near.

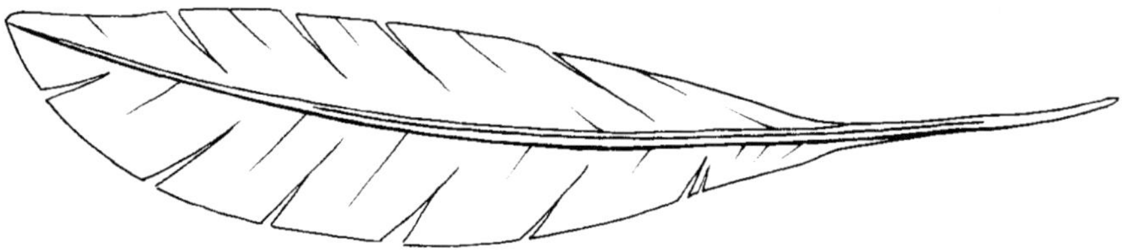

My Dad says he's a Loony

My dad just warned me off. "He's a Loony!
Now keep away from him, or else, you hear?"
I heard. This must be a Grown Up to fear!
"Shouts like a loony, Head's on the Moony
His knives and forks are totally Spoony!
Built this Ship on a hill!" Dad slurped his beer,
"From doors and bits of rubbish! It's quite clear,"
He shouted, "That his brain's a bit puny!"

At night, I dream of a Ship in green grass....
And if the rain sang, if hills turned to sea,
I'd fly from Drinking Dad, his Stinking Glass.
We'd slip off the land, dive over each tree
Sailing deep valleys, Sun bright as brass,
Just Noah the Wiser and ten-year-old-me.

The Safest Place in the World

Once I climbed
To the top of a tree
Low lay the town,
Spread like a sea.

Branches bent
To make a seat,
The world swam by
Beneath my feet.

Rooves shone out,
Their blue-black tiles
Like scaly fish
With chimney smiles.

I had clambered
Out of a box,
A lid of leaves,
And me the fox...

No bullies to hunt me,
Where birds sing clear
I'm king of the wind!
I banish fear!

The sun ran home
And stars fell out
"Time for dinner!"
I heard Mum shout.

I slid down the slide
Built from bark
Out of the sky
And into the dark.

Bob the Yob
(The Boy without a Brain)

I'm an ice-cream bombe,
That goes with a bang,
But don't call me sweet,
'Cos I'm one of the gang.

I crumple Coke cans
With my bare fist,
I'm a Curly-Wurly,
I'm round the twist.

I'm a window-breaker
I'm a smash, I'm a hit!
But I can't understand
Why you think I'm a twit?

No I ain't scared of no-one
{unless your brother's about}
But if you're smaller than me,
You'd better watch out!

I'm cool as a lollipop
That no-one can lick.
I'm a house on fire,
I'm thick as a brick.

Without my gang,
I'm a pod without peas,
I go all mushy
And weak at the knees.

But there ain't no situation
That I can't handle,
I hang around doorways,
I'm unhinged, I'm a vandal!

And our last Story Tonight

And our last story tonight....
The Earth has been taken to hospital!
Mrs Smith of 93 Duggan Street, Dulham,
Was a neighbour:

"I just popped out for five minutes,
And when I came back,
There she was,
Lying on the floor!
Of course it was none of my business,
But she had a bit of difficulty breathing!
Naturally,
I called the ambulance straightaway
And they took her off....
I didn't know her very well,
Well, you know what it's like these days,
And my eyes aren't what they used to be."

Said Mrs Smith of 93 Duggan Street, Dulham.

Any witnesses are asked to come forward,
Though police have dismissed allegations
That pollution is to blame as, *"A load of old rubbish."*

And now for our weekly *'spot the crisp-packet-in-the-hedge'* competition...

Last Night, I saw the City Breathing

Last night, I saw the City breathing
Great Gusts of people,
Rushing in and
Puffing out
Of Station's singing mouths.

Last night, I saw the City laughing.
Take-Aways got the giggles,
Cinemas split their sides,
And Living Rooms completely creased themselves!

Last night, I saw the City dancing.
Shadows were cheek to cheek with brick walls,
Trains wiggled their hips all over the place,
And the trees
In the breeze,
Put on a show for an audience of windows!

Last night, I saw the city starving,
Snaking Avenue smacked her lips
And swallowed seven roundabouts!
Fat office blocks got stuffed with light
And gloated over empty parking lots.

Last night, I saw the City crying.
Cracked windows poured falling stars
And the streets were paved with mirrors.

Last night, I saw the City sleeping
Roads night-dreamed,
Street Lamps quietly boasted,
'WHEN I GROW UP, I'M GOING TO BE A STAR!'
And the Wind,
Like a cat,
Snoozed in the nooks of roofs.

Rush Hour Rhythm

rush
i must
i must rush
sorry
i must rush
do up my tie
tied up in business,
no time to stop
gotta hoppit

rush
i must
i must rush
sorry, gotta go,
gotta rush
gotta lotta rush
gotta lotta bottle rush rush rush...
angry faces all in soup
sardine soup, gloupity gloop
boil it up!
boil it up!
boil in the bag burst
BEEP! BEEP! BEEP!
Out of my way, gonna mash you up!
gonna gonna gonna, you'll be a goner
gonna do you, do you how do you do? do do do, do-doos!
WHAT A MESS!
grown ups in ten car pile-ups!

rush rush rush
gotta get a lot of dosh dosh dosh
gotta do a job
gotta do a big job
big jobs! little jobs!
job job job-jam
caught in a job jam
clock in
tick tock tick tock clockwork
in work
i'm really into work
clock out
get out
get out of my way
BEEP! BEEP! BEEP!
time for sleep sleep sleep
got the time?
No I haven't got the time
never ever be time
for once upon a time
cos now we gotta rush
into the rhythm of the cars
cos now we gotta rush
into the rhythm of the cars
cos now we gotta rush
into the rhythm of the cars

sorry
gotta go
gotta rush
gotta lotta rush
gotta lotta bottle rush
rush hour
crush hour
hush hour

Ballad of the Trees

In your words, I am an Oak tree,
And I have been here a hundred years or more.
They tried to put me away in an old people's home,
But I'm still hanging about in the street like a tramp,
The earth is a good bed
And my blanket the wide sky.

Once,
I was round, small as your thumb
Until my mother dropped me,
Just like that.
I fell to the ground,
A dream inside a seed,
Waiting.

Then,
This street was stripped of its bark
And underneath lay the muddy drover's path.
Horses ploughed your classroom and
Wheat grew between your desks.
It is so easy to forget.

Now,
In your words,
I am grown old.
The concrete hides me away,
And the street tries to run me over.
I wrap myself in bark
Against this biting wind.

But if you stop
And listen,
I shall promise to sing you a song of leaves
And if you dream,
Dream the cold hearted cities away, away
Dream the cold hearted cities away.

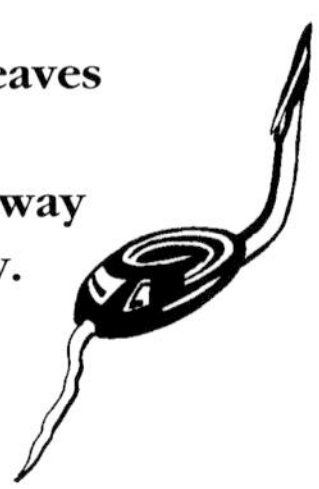

The Milk Cup

My baby sister crawls around,
Mum and Dad think she'll go far,
The crowd of uncles oohing and aahing,
She gets more kisses than a football star!

At the moment, she's in training,
And when she dribbles, they go dotty.
Her coach, {my mum!}, she screams with delight,
"The Nappies have lost! Hurrah for the Potty!"

When she throws a skilful tantrum,
It's loud enough to wake the dead!
This is the penalty of having a sister,
The ref blows his whistle, she's sent off {to bed!}

I'm the player they all ignore,
When she's foul, I get the blame
They've chucked me from Division Fun,
Gimme a transfer! I hate this game!

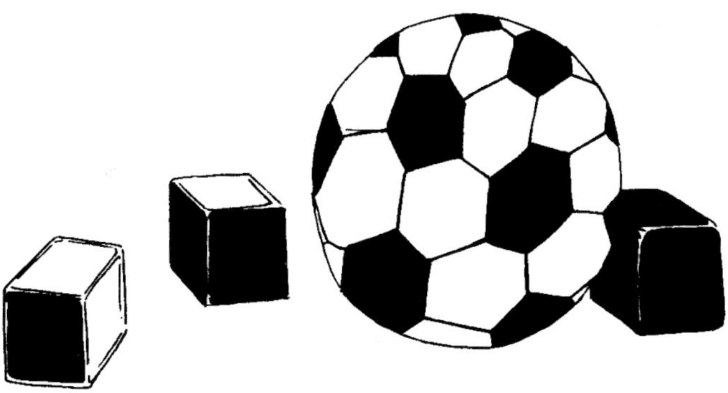

Street Signs

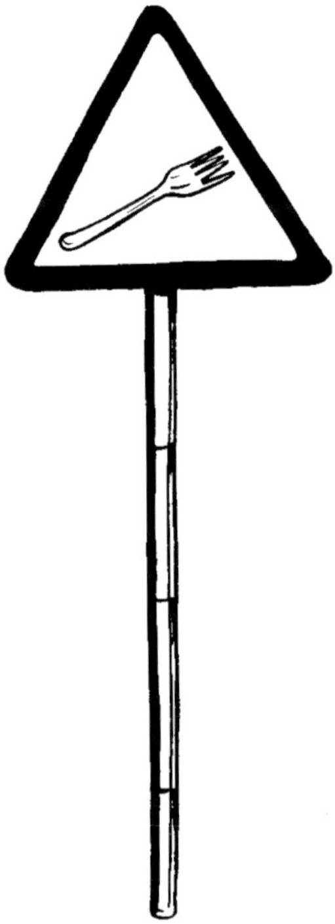

DEAD SLOW CHILDREN!
And so I slowed,
Hundreds were crawling
Down the middle of the road!

FORK AHEAD!
I rubbed my eyes
A fifty foot fork
Pronging the skies!
I think I'm going
Round the bend!
There was a sausage
The size of a house
On the end!

HEAVY PLANT CROSSING!
I fought with my brolly
As a dastardly daffodil
Said, *"Give us your lolly!"*

A HUMP BRIDGE!
Was next, I stopped with a bump,
The bridge had run off,
It had got the hump!

DIVERSION AHEAD!
I'd be home quite soon
First left, then right,
I arrived... on the moon!

The Mansion

(For the children of High Ercall school, Shropshire)

The house stood still like a solitary crane
In a pool of deep green grass,
The windows dark as thundered rain,
Rooms all drowned in glass.

Shadow hen, now come to roost,
It pecked and gobbled the light,
Here, the house is only host,
To the visiting fox of night.

House that once held charm and chime
Now a bricked up box of air.
The thief has come and stolen time,
The silence dies, there's no-one there.

This house a washed-up, lonely shell
On the grey and windswept lea.
But cup your ear and listen well
To the hiss of the far off sea.

Night

***O**nion Moon*
In a bowl of night;
Sliver of silver,
Garnish of light.

Day

Onion sun
Peels night away;
Layers of dark
Unravelling day.

A batty tongue twister

The Cat sat on the mat

SEE HOW FAST YOU CAN SAY THIS!

Pat had a flat
And a hat.
On the hat sat a rat
On the rat sat a bat
With a bat
(A cricket bat).

Bat with a bat
On a rat
On a hat
On Pat
In a flat.

One day,
In the flat
Came a gnat,
Saw the bat
Bit the bat
What was that?
The bat spat
Hit the gnat
With the bat
Went splat!

That was the end
Of That!

The Noun with no Name

It was a Dark and Gloomy Paragraph.

We followed the Noun with No Name

Through a

Long

And

Winding

Sentence

Until

At last

We came to a full stop.

He had gone!

Leaving only an exclamation mark!

This was a job for:

The Verb Without A Clause......

A Headbanging Poem

dedicated to tall and clumsy people throughout the world

Oh my head is a right old banger,
I'm tall as a tree, you see.
It goes bump in the night,
And scars the living daylights out of me.

Oh my head is a right old banger!
It's driving me head-banging mad!
My forehead keeps beating up door-frames
And my nose is a battered crash-pad.

Oh my head is right old banger!
I'm always heading for a crash,
Why must I make a meal of it
And end up as bangers and mash?

Oh my head is a right old banger!
One bang and I start to see stars!
Then I turn dizzy as a catherine wheel
And my eyes are bumper cars.

Oh why is my head an old banger?
This banging's a pain in the head.
One day, I'll end up with one bang too many,
And be banged up in heaven, quite dead!

PLEASE DO
NOT FEED
THE ANIMALS

Gorilla

A gorilla sits
And stares at the wall.

Big,
Black,
A brain that is enormous;
Pools of eyes
Drowning in sadness.

The gorilla in the zoo
Is looking at you.
Will you tap the glass?
Try to make him laugh?

Ten foot by ten foot
Of sculptured concrete
For his huge feet.

He dreams of leaves
Bigger than a newspaper
And walking through greenness for a hundred miles in a straight line without stopping.

Now he walks a hundred miles
Ten
Foot
At
A
Time.

The Rubbishman

I'm the Rubbish-Man,
Prince of Plastic, King of Tin Can.
People say I'm disgusting,
But the children are so trusting
When I rip {*or do they throw?*}
Such sweet wrappers out of their hands
To scatter them brightly across the lands.

I am the Reveller of Rags,
Emperor of Empty Shopping Bags.

Yes! I'm the Rubbish Man!
Catch me, Collar me, Collect me if you can.
It's me who stole into your sleep,
Took your mattress soft and deep.
Now, I'm coiled up, comfortably rusting by the Rubbish Stream
As She slips her way through the city's dark dream.

Oh! I'm the Rubbish Man!
Rubbing out wishes as only I can.
I made the blocks that burn the sky
And if you dare to ask me why,
I'll say it's my job, it's what I do.
Then will I dance The Rubbish Dance for you.

For, I'm the Rubbish Man!
Bin me, Bag me, Beat me if you can,
But together we'll dance all days away
And Darkness, my friend, shall come to stay.

Hey Diddle Diddle

Wash your ears! Mum said.
So I took them off,
And stuck them in the washing machine.

Clean your room! Dad said.
So I rolled it up,
And shook it out of the window.

Make the breakfast! My brother said
So I did -
With bits of balsa wood and modelling glue.

Feed the Cat, My Auntie said,
So I fed him...
To the dog!

Take your time! Dad said.
So I packed up the clocks
And flew off to Mars
Where the days fly by,
Wearing nothing but stars!

A Tidy Poem

Right then! It's time to tidy up the sky!
That's enough of your cheek! Don't ask me why!
I have told you a thousand times today
To put every one of those clouds away!
I've said it once, and I'll say it again,
You're just not old enough to play with rain!
Hey! You heard me! Leave those mountains alone!
They're sharp, unlike you, with a brain thick as stone!

And I don't care if you're a God in Heaven,
No pudding for you and bed at seven!

A Farewell Ode

We've come at last to the final page,
I hope I've served you well
And that this little interlude
Has cast a lyric spell.

It's over now, it's done between us!
It's time to go. (I guess!)
It's the finale, the last full stop,
But I will miss you so (Oh yes!)

Now, if you liked it very much,
Please scream and snort and shout.
And if you didn't, then beware,
For I shall find you out,

'Cos I'm the Poet with a pen,
That's sharper than the sword,
I'm a Cut-throat Versifier;
And if you're getting bored,

I'll mash you with my metaphors,
My rap will tap your toes,
For I'm the Naughty *Villain*-elle
Who steals away your woes.

So drop your boredom in a lake,
And set your thinking free;
Find the forest of ideas
And climb the Poet-Tree.

Biography

Andrew Fusek Peters is an Anglo-Czech writer, storyteller, presenter, poet and didjeridu player with many years experience of working in the media and education. Andrew has been a member of the Poetry Society's *Poets-In-Schools* scheme since 1990.

His work has featured on *Poetry Please, Talking Poetry, Anderson Country, Megamix, Kaleidoscope, The Big Breakfast* and *Blue Peter*. He was a presenter/writer for BBC1's poetry series *Wham! Bam! Strawberry Jam!* Andrew won the Radio 4/Arts Council *Write Out Loud Award* and has recorded the poetic comedy-drama *Mr Acoustic* for Radio 4. He is currently writing/presenting for a new Channel 4 series *Poetry In Motion.*

He has poems in the following anthologies: The Radio 4/Poetry Society YOUNG POETRY PACK, THE FABER BOOK OF FIRST VERSE, CUSTARD PIE by Macmillan, and a Stanley Thornes education pack.

Collections include:
WORDWHYS (Sherbourne) "Andrew Peters is a one-off. His spellbinding performances combine atmospheric telling of traditional tales, the haunting and powerful didjeridu and his funny but thought-provoking poems. It's a stunning combination!" Viv Beeby, producer Talking Poetry
THE WEATHER'S GETTING VERSE (Sherbourne)
"Boisterous...good fun...strongly produced and well illustrated." TES
"Thought-provoking and fun...should take your classroom by storm!" Alison Combes, Poetry Soc Ed Officer (on the Poetry Society Schools Recommended Reading List and short listed for Arts Council Writer's Awards).
His first collection for adults - WHEN I COME TO THE DARK COUNTRY, is published by Abbotsford Publishing.
He is the editor of SHEEP DON'T GO TO SCHOOL (A Bloodaxe Book of East European Children's Poetry) which won an Arts Council European translation grant.

After the death of his brother Mark from AIDS, a collection of their poetry, MAY THE ANGELS BE WITH US was published by Shropshire County Council. This book gained national acclaim, with features in the Guardian, TES and on Kaleidoscope. "Your poems make me wish that I had known your brother. But then his own work triumphantly survives him." Sir Ian McKellen "A powerful collection" TES "very moving poems...I was moved to tears." Kaleidoscope. "I have been deeply moved by the poems" Alastair Niven. "This book is more than just a collection of poetry. It is a testament of love. It is unique." Brian Patten.

He has also written THE BAREFOOT BOOK OF STRANGE & SPOOKY STORIES, SALT IS SWEETER THAN GOLD (Barefoot) and reading scheme storybooks for Ginn and HarperCollins.

Notes on the Illustrator

Danny Bradford was born in Londonderry in 1964, he studied at the Bangor School of Art and graduated from Sheffield Polytechnic in 1986. He lives with his family in a converted railway cattle truck on a small-holding near Welshpool. With the help of his wife he attempts to be self sufficient through a large garden with pigs, chickens, rabbits, dogs and a ferret. In between caring for his family and animals he draws pictures.

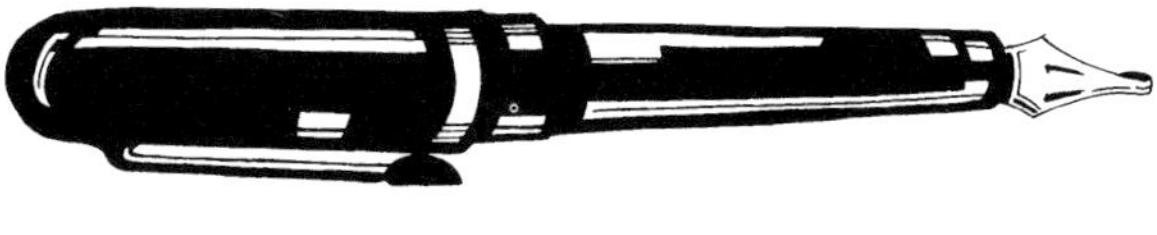